AI for Content Creators:
From Idea to Execution, AI-Powered Tools for Creative Projects

Jamie Tyler

Copyright © 2024 Jamie Tyler
All rights reserved.

No part of this publication may be reproduced, distributed, or transmitted in any form or by any means, including photocopying, recording, or other electronic or mechanical methods, without the prior written permission of the author, except in the case of brief quotations embodied in critical reviews and certain other non-commercial uses permitted by copyright law.

Table of Contents

Introduction

- Why AI is Transforming Content Creation
- How to Use This Book

Chapter 1: The Basics of AI in Content Creation

- Understanding Core AI Technologies
- Ethical Considerations and Limitations

Chapter 2: AI for Writers

- Tools for Enhanced Writing and Editing
- Practical Applications and Tips

Chapter 3: AI for Video Editing

- Automating Video Production Tasks
- Improving Creativity and Efficiency

Chapter 4: AI for Graphic Design

- AI Tools for Design and Illustration
- Enhancing Visual Content Creation

Chapter 5: AI in Social Media Content Creation

- Planning and Automating Social Media Content
- Optimizing Engagement with AI

Chapter 6: Collaborative AI Tools for Teams

- Streamlining Team Workflows with AI
- Enhancing Communication and Creativity

Chapter 7: Overcoming Challenges in AI Content Creation

- Maintaining Authenticity and Ethics
- Avoiding Over-Reliance on AI

Chapter 8: The Future of AI in Content Creation

- Emerging Technologies and Trends
- Preparing for the Future of Creativity

Conclusion

- Embracing AI as a Creative Partner & Final Thoughts of Future Content Creation

Introduction: Embracing the AI Revolution in Content Creation

Welcome to the Future of Creativity

In a world where technology evolves at lightning speed, staying ahead in the creative industry means more than just keeping up with trends. It requires embracing new tools and technologies that can enhance and transform your creative process. This book, **"AI for Content Creators: How to Leverage AI Tools for Writing, Video Editing, and Graphic Design,"** is your guide to navigating this exciting new frontier where artificial intelligence and human creativity intersect.

Why AI Matters in Content Creation

The rise of AI in content creation is not just a technological shift; it's a creative revolution. AI tools are now capable of generating text, editing videos, designing graphics, and even crafting social media strategies—tasks that once required specialized skills and significant time investment. For content creators, this means new opportunities to streamline workflows, explore innovative ideas, and reach wider audiences.

But AI is more than just a tool for efficiency. It's a powerful partner that can inspire new forms of creativity. By automating routine tasks, AI frees creators to focus on what they do best: telling compelling stories, designing stunning visuals, and crafting memorable experiences.

What You'll Learn in This Book

This book is designed to be a comprehensive guide for content creators of all kinds—writers, designers, video editors, marketers, and more—who want to harness the power of AI to enhance their creative processes. Each chapter delves into a specific area of content creation, providing practical tips, tool recommendations, and exercises to help you integrate AI into your work.

- **Chapter 1: The Basics of AI in Content Creation** explores foundational AI technologies like Natural Language Processing (NLP), machine learning, and computer vision, setting the stage for understanding how these tools can transform your workflow.
- **Chapter 2: AI for Writers** introduces AI-driven writing tools that assist with everything from content generation and grammar checking to creative ideation, helping writers overcome writer's block and enhance their craft.
- **Chapter 3: AI for Video Editing** covers AI-powered tools that automate tasks like scene detection, video summarization, and voiceovers, enabling video creators to produce professional-quality content more efficiently.
- **Chapter 4: AI for Graphic Design** explores how AI can aid in creating stunning visuals, from automated design generation to image enhancement and logo creation, making high-quality design accessible to everyone.
- **Chapter 5: AI in Social Media Content Creation** focuses on tools that help plan, create, and schedule social media content, optimizing engagement and streamlining the process of maintaining a consistent online presence.
- **Chapter 6: Collaborative AI Tools for Teams** examines AI solutions that facilitate teamwork, real-time editing, and project management, enhancing collaboration among content creation teams.
- **Chapter 7: Overcoming Challenges in AI Content Creation** addresses common challenges, such as maintaining a unique voice and navigating ethical implications, offering strategies for integrating AI into your creative workflow without losing your personal touch.
- **Chapter 8: The Future of AI in Content Creation** looks ahead to emerging technologies and trends that will shape the future of content creation, inspiring readers to stay ahead of the curve and continue innovating with AI.

Who This Book Is For

Whether you're a seasoned professional looking to incorporate AI into your existing workflow or a newcomer curious about the possibilities of AI in creative fields, this book offers something for everyone. It's designed for:

- **Writers** seeking to enhance their storytelling with AI-driven tools that assist with drafting, editing, and idea generation.
- **Graphic Designers** wanting to explore how AI can streamline their design process, from automated layouts to advanced image manipulation.
- **Video Creators** looking for tools that can speed up editing and improve the quality of their videos.
- **Social Media Managers** who want to optimize their content strategy and automate scheduling and engagement.
- **Marketing Teams and Agencies** interested in using AI to improve collaboration and scale content production.
- **Creatives and Innovators** eager to explore the cutting-edge of AI technology and its impact on the arts and media.

How to Use This Book

This book is structured to be both informative and practical. Each chapter includes detailed explanations of AI tools, real-world examples, and hands-on exercises to help you apply what you've learned. While you can read it from cover to cover, feel free to jump to the chapters that interest you the most.

The Creative Potential of AI: A New Chapter Begins

As we stand at the threshold of this new era, it's clear that AI is not just a tool but a catalyst for change. It challenges us to think differently, to explore new possibilities, and to push the boundaries of what we can create. The future of content creation is not about choosing between human and machine but finding new ways to collaborate and innovate together.

We hope this book inspires you to experiment with AI, embrace new creative possibilities, and discover how technology can elevate your work to new heights. Welcome to the future of content creation—your creative journey with AI starts here.

Chapter 1: The Basics of AI in Content Creation

Understanding AI and Its Role in Content Creation

Artificial Intelligence (AI) is not just a technical tool for data scientists; it's rapidly becoming an essential partner for content creators across the globe. Whether you're a writer looking to streamline your drafting process, a video editor aiming to cut down on repetitive tasks, or a graphic designer exploring new creative possibilities, AI can help you work smarter and unleash your creativity. But to harness these tools effectively, it's important to understand the technologies that power them and the contexts in which they thrive.

Key AI Technologies in Content Creation

Natural Language Processing (NLP): Enhancing Written Content

Imagine you're staring at a blank page, struggling to start a blog post. This is where AI tools powered by Natural Language Processing (NLP) come in handy. For instance, tools like **OpenAI's ChatGPT** can generate opening paragraphs based on a few keywords or topics you provide. You might type, "Write an introduction about how AI is changing graphic design," and in seconds, you have a draft to build upon. This can help overcome writer's block and spark new ideas.

Tip for Writers: Don't treat the AI-generated text as your final output. Use it as a starting point, then refine and add your unique voice and perspective. This ensures the content remains authentic and true to your style.

Exercise:

1. Choose a topic for a blog post.
2. Use ChatGPT to generate an introductory paragraph.

3. Edit and expand the paragraph, adding your own insights and personal anecdotes.

Machine Learning: Personalizing Content Strategy

Have you ever wondered how platforms like Netflix know exactly what shows to recommend or how e-commerce sites suggest products you didn't even know you wanted? That's machine learning at work, using your behavior to predict your preferences. Content creators can leverage similar ML-based tools to tailor their strategies.

For example, **HubSpot's Content Strategy Tool** can analyze your website's content and suggest topics that resonate with your audience based on engagement metrics and search trends. This means you can plan your content calendar around what your audience is most likely to find valuable, rather than guessing.

Practical Use Case: A freelance writer might use this tool to identify high-traffic topics in their niche and pitch more relevant article ideas to clients, boosting their chances of acceptance and readership.

Exercise:

1. Use a content strategy tool like HubSpot to analyze your current content.
2. List the top three suggested topics and create an outline for each.
3. Plan a content calendar for the next month based on these insights.

Computer Vision: Revolutionizing Visual Content Creation

If you've ever struggled with tedious tasks like removing backgrounds from images or creating complex visual effects, computer vision tools can be a game-changer. Take **Remove.bg**, for instance—it allows you to remove backgrounds from images with a single click. This is incredibly useful for creating product images, social media graphics, or even personal branding visuals without needing advanced Photoshop skills.

Tip for Designers: Use computer vision tools to automate repetitive tasks, but don't shy away from adding your own creative touch. AI can handle the heavy lifting, leaving you free to focus on more complex design elements.

Exercise:

1. Upload a product photo to Remove.bg and remove the background.
2. Use Canva or Adobe Spark to design a social media post using this image, experimenting with different layouts and text overlays.

Ethical Implications of AI in Creative Fields

While AI offers numerous advantages, it's crucial to consider the ethical implications of its use in creative industries. Authenticity and originality are key concerns. For example, tools like **QuillBot**, an AI paraphrasing tool, can help you rephrase sentences to avoid plagiarism. However, over-reliance on such tools can blur the line between genuine creativity and automated content generation.

Real-World Scenario: A student might use QuillBot to rewrite a passage from a research article, but if they don't understand the material, the resulting content could be shallow or misleading. It's essential to balance AI assistance with thorough research and personal input.

Exercise:

1. Select a paragraph from an article related to your field of interest.

2. Use QuillBot to rephrase it, then write a short paragraph explaining the key points in your own words.

Data privacy is another critical issue. Many AI tools, like chatbots or recommendation engines, rely on user data to function effectively. Creators need to ensure they are transparent about data usage and compliant with privacy regulations. Tools like **Ghostery** can help you understand what data is being collected on your website and how to minimize it.

Limitations of AI in Content Creation

AI tools, while powerful, are not perfect. They can struggle with complex creative tasks that require deep contextual understanding or emotional nuance. For example, while **Jasper (formerly Jarvis)** can generate marketing copy quickly, it may produce repetitive or generic content if the input prompt is vague.

Pro Tip: When using AI for content generation, be as specific as possible with your prompts. Instead of "Write about AI in marketing," try "Write about how AI chatbots can improve customer service for small businesses." This will help the AI produce more targeted and useful content.

Exercise:

1. Choose a broad topic like "digital marketing."
2. Refine this topic into three specific prompts and use Jasper to generate a paragraph for each.
3. Compare the outputs and identify how specificity affects the quality of the content.

The Human-AI Collaboration: Blending Creativity with Efficiency

The true power of AI in content creation lies in collaboration. Think of AI as a creative assistant that can handle repetitive tasks, provide data-driven insights, and even suggest new creative directions. For instance, a YouTuber might use **Adobe Premiere Pro's** AI features to automate video cuts and scene detection, then focus on adding unique voiceovers and personal anecdotes.

Workflow Example:

1. Use **BuzzSumo** to identify trending topics in your niche.
2. Draft initial content with **Jasper** or **Copy.ai**.
3. Edit for clarity and style using **Grammarly** and **Hemingway Editor**.
4. Design visuals in **Canva** or **Adobe Spark**.
5. Optimize for SEO using tools like **Yoast SEO** or **Clearscope**.

Exercise:

1. Choose a content piece (blog, video, or social media post).
2. Go through each step of the workflow, using the suggested AI tools.
3. Reflect on how the tools improved efficiency and where you added your unique input.

Conclusion

In this chapter, we've explored how AI technologies like NLP, machine learning, and computer vision are transforming content creation. By integrating these tools thoughtfully into your creative process, you can save time, enhance quality, and focus on what truly matters—bringing your unique voice and vision to life.

Chapter 2: AI for Writers

Introduction: Revolutionizing the Writing Process with AI

For writers, crafting compelling content involves more than just putting words on paper. It's about conveying ideas effectively, engaging the audience, and maintaining a consistent voice. However, the creative process can be time-consuming and mentally taxing. This is where AI tools come into play, assisting writers in everything from brainstorming and drafting to editing and optimizing their work. Many content creators have already embraced these tools, and their experiences offer valuable insights into how AI can elevate your writing process.

The Evolving Role of AI in Writing

AI is reshaping the writing landscape, making repetitive tasks more manageable and providing creative support. For instance, marketing consultant and content creator **Ann Handley** notes, "AI is a powerful co-pilot. It helps me with idea generation and gives me a starting point for my content. It's not a replacement for my creativity, but it helps me get over the initial hump when I'm staring at a blank page." Ann's experience highlights a common use case for AI—overcoming writer's block and kickstarting the creative process.

AI Tools for Writing: An In-Depth Look

1. Jasper (formerly Jarvis): The Creative Copy Companion

Jasper is designed to assist writers in generating high-quality content quickly. Many content creators have turned to Jasper to streamline their workflows. **Hana LaRock**, a freelance writer, shares her experience: "Jasper helped me double my productivity. I used to spend hours crafting the perfect intro for my blog posts.

Now, I use Jasper to create the first draft, and I refine it from there. It saves me at least an hour on every article."

Practical Use Case: Imagine you're tasked with writing a blog post titled "The Future of Remote Work." After feeding this topic into Jasper, it generates an introduction like this:

"Remote work is no longer a trend—it's the new normal. As businesses adapt to this shift, they're rethinking everything from communication tools to office space. But what does the future hold? In this post, we'll explore emerging trends and what they mean for workers and employers alike."

You can then build on this foundation, adding your insights and examples.

Exercise:

1. Choose a topic related to your industry or interest.
2. Use Jasper to generate an introduction and two supporting paragraphs.
3. Review the generated content and expand upon it with personal anecdotes or research findings.

2. Grammarly and Hemingway Editor: Your AI Editorial Team

Editing and proofreading are essential steps in the writing process, and AI can make these tasks much easier. Content strategist **Joe Lazauskas** mentions, "Grammarly is my go-to tool for catching those pesky typos and ensuring my content is polished before I hit publish. It's like having an extra set of eyes that never gets tired."

Hemingway Editor, on the other hand, focuses on readability. It highlights complex sentences and passive voice, making it easier to simplify your writing. These tools are invaluable for writers who want to ensure their content is clear and professional.

Pro Tip: Use Grammarly first to catch any grammatical issues, then refine your text with Hemingway to improve clarity and readability.

Exercise:

1. Write a 300-word piece on any topic.
2. Run it through Grammarly and make the suggested changes.
3. Paste the revised text into Hemingway Editor and adjust according to the tool's recommendations, aiming for a readability score of Grade 7 or lower.

3. Frase and BuzzSumo: Mastering Content Research

Research is a critical part of writing, but it can be time-consuming. Tools like Frase and BuzzSumo streamline the process by providing insights into trending topics, popular questions, and competitor content. **Neil Patel**, a digital marketing expert, says, "BuzzSumo is an essential part of my content strategy. It helps me identify what's trending and what people are talking about, so I can create content that's relevant and timely."

Practical Use Case: Suppose you're writing an article on "Sustainable Fashion." Using Frase, you can quickly gather insights such as:

- Top questions people ask about sustainable fashion (e.g., "What are the benefits of sustainable fashion?")
- Key subtopics to cover (e.g., "Eco-friendly fabrics," "Slow fashion vs. fast fashion")
- A suggested outline based on top-performing articles.

Exercise:

1. Pick a topic and use Frase to generate a content outline.
2. Research each subtopic using BuzzSumo to find trending articles and key influencers in that space.
3. Use these insights to create a detailed outline or first draft of your article.

Case Studies: AI in Action

Case Study 1: Boosting Blog Production with AI

A digital marketing agency needed to scale its content production to meet client demand but struggled with maintaining quality. They integrated Jasper into their workflow, using it to generate first drafts for blog posts. This allowed their writers to focus on refining and optimizing content rather than starting from scratch. The result? A 40% increase in content output and improved client satisfaction.

Takeaway: AI can be a powerful ally in scaling content production without sacrificing quality, provided that human writers remain involved in the creative and editorial process.

Case Study 2: Enhancing Creative Writing with AI

An independent author used **Sudowrite**, an AI tool designed for fiction writers, to help overcome writer's block during the drafting of a fantasy novel. Sudowrite suggested unique plot twists and character developments based on the author's initial notes. While not every suggestion was used, the tool provided fresh perspectives that inspired new directions for the story.

Takeaway: AI can serve as a brainstorming partner, offering creative ideas that push writers out of their comfort zones and into unexplored narrative territories.

Quote from Author: "Sudowrite didn't write my book for me, but it did help me see my story from a new angle. It was like having a brainstorming session with a creative friend who never runs out of ideas," the author remarked.

Practical Tips for Writers Using AI

1. **Start with a Strong Prompt**: The quality of AI-generated content largely depends on the input. Craft clear, detailed prompts to guide the AI toward producing relevant and coherent content.
2. **Edit Thoroughly**: AI tools are not infallible. Always review and revise AI-generated content to ensure accuracy, tone, and coherence.
3. **Use AI for Repetitive Tasks**: Automate mundane tasks like grammar checking, keyword research, and content ideation, allowing you to focus on more creative aspects of writing.

Quote from Content Creator: "AI is great for getting the basics down, but the real magic happens in the editing phase. That's where you can really make the content your own," says **Julia McCoy**, a content marketing expert.

Overcoming Common Challenges

1. Maintaining a Unique Voice

One of the biggest concerns with AI-generated content is the potential loss of a writer's unique voice. To mitigate this, use AI tools primarily for drafting and research, then infuse your personality and style during the editing phase. Remember, AI should enhance your creativity, not replace it.

Exercise:

1. Write a short paragraph about your favorite book or movie.
2. Use an AI tool to generate a similar paragraph.

3. Compare the two and blend the best elements of both to create a final version that retains your voice but benefits from the AI's structure or insights.

2. Avoiding Over-Reliance on AI

While AI can be a great assistant, it's important not to become overly dependent. Ensure that you're still honing your own writing skills by setting aside time for writing without AI tools. This will help you maintain a strong foundation and use AI as a complementary tool rather than a crutch.

Exercise:

1. Spend 15 minutes each day writing without any AI assistance.
2. Choose a different prompt each day, such as "Describe a memorable place" or "Write a letter to your future self."
3. After a week, review your progress and identify areas where your natural writing skills have improved.

Conclusion: Embracing AI as a Writing Partner

AI tools are revolutionizing the writing process, offering new ways to generate ideas, draft content, and refine text. By integrating these tools into your workflow, you can enhance productivity and creativity, freeing up more time to focus on what you do best: telling compelling stories and sharing valuable insights.

In the next chapter, we'll explore how AI can transform video editing, from automating tedious tasks to creating engaging content optimized for various platforms. Get ready to dive into the world of AI-enhanced video creation!

Chapter 3: AI for Video Editing

Introduction: Transforming Video Creation with AI

Video content is king in today's digital landscape, with platforms like YouTube, TikTok, and Instagram driving engagement through dynamic, visual storytelling. Yet, producing high-quality video content is often time-consuming and requires a significant investment in editing. This is where AI-powered tools are making a significant impact. By automating complex tasks and simplifying workflows, AI enables creators to focus more on storytelling and creative direction. In this chapter, we'll explore how AI is revolutionizing video editing, from automating mundane tasks to enhancing creativity and accessibility.

AI-Powered Video Editing: The Essentials

AI in video editing goes beyond simple automation; it leverages advanced algorithms to understand and manipulate video content intelligently. Whether it's identifying key scenes, suggesting transitions, or even generating entire video summaries, AI tools are helping editors create professional-quality content faster and more efficiently.

One of the most transformative aspects of AI in video editing is its ability to handle repetitive tasks. Imagine you've shot hours of footage for a documentary. Sifting through this to find the best takes is not only tedious but also mentally exhausting. Tools like **Adobe Premiere Pro's Auto Reframe** feature use AI to automatically detect and crop shots for different aspect ratios, saving countless hours of manual work. Similarly, **Magisto** uses AI to analyze video content, selecting the most compelling segments and seamlessly editing them together with music and effects.

Tip for Editors: Use AI to handle the heavy lifting of organizing and rough-cutting your footage. This frees you up to focus on the more nuanced aspects of storytelling, like pacing and emotion.

Automating Tedious Tasks with AI

1. Scene Detection and Video Summarization

One of the most time-consuming tasks in video editing is identifying and categorizing different scenes, especially when working with long recordings or multiple cameras. AI tools like **Descript** offer automatic scene detection, breaking down footage into individual segments based on dialogue and visual changes. This feature is particularly useful for creators working on interviews or webinars, as it allows them to jump directly to specific points in the conversation.

Exercise:

1. Upload a lengthy interview or webinar recording to Descript.
2. Use the scene detection feature to create a visual timeline of key moments.
3. Use this breakdown to create a shorter, more engaging highlight reel.

2. Automated Voiceovers and Subtitling

Adding voiceovers and subtitles can be a labor-intensive process, especially for content creators who produce videos regularly. AI tools like **Sonix** and **Rev.ai** can transcribe audio tracks automatically, making it easy to add accurate subtitles to your videos. For voiceovers, tools like **Lovo** offer high-quality AI-generated voices in multiple languages and accents, allowing creators to localize their content for different audiences.

Practical Use Case: Imagine you're creating an explainer video for a global audience. Instead of recording separate voiceovers in different languages, you can use Lovo to generate voiceovers in

Spanish, French, and Mandarin from the same script. This not only saves time but also broadens your content's reach.

Exercise:

1. Write a short script for an explainer video.
2. Use Lovo to generate voiceovers in at least two different languages.
3. Use the voiceovers to create multilingual versions of your video.

Enhancing Creativity with AI

1. Intelligent Effects and Transitions

AI tools are not just about automation—they can also spark creativity by suggesting new ways to enhance your videos. **Filmora's AI Portrait** feature, for example, can automatically remove backgrounds, leaving you with a clean subject that you can place into any setting. This is particularly useful for creators who lack professional green screen setups but still want that effect.

Similarly, tools like **Runway ML** offer a suite of AI-powered effects, such as background removal, colorization, and even "rotoscoping" (a labor-intensive technique traditionally used to create matte effects in film). These capabilities enable creators to experiment with professional-level effects without the need for expensive software or hours of manual work.

Exercise:

1. Shoot a short video against a plain background.
2. Use Filmora's AI Portrait feature to remove the background and experiment with different virtual settings.
3. Try adding a few AI-generated effects from Runway ML, like motion tracking or color correction, to elevate the visual quality of your video.

2. Automating Video Personalization

Personalization is key to engaging audiences on platforms like YouTube and Instagram. AI can help tailor content for different viewers by creating multiple versions of the same video with slight variations. Tools like **Veed.io** and **Content Samurai** can automatically generate different intros, outros, or calls to action based on user demographics or platform requirements.

Practical Use Case: A YouTuber might create personalized end screens thanking subscribers by name. Using Veed.io, they can automate this process, generating hundreds of personalized video versions in minutes.

Exercise:

1. Create a basic video with a customizable section (e.g., "Thank you, [Name], for watching!").
2. Use Veed.io to generate different versions of this video for different audience segments (e.g., specific callouts for Patreon supporters or long-time subscribers).
3. Upload the personalized videos to your preferred platform and track engagement metrics.

AI Tools for Optimizing Video Content

1. Video SEO Optimization

Creating great content is only half the battle; ensuring it reaches your audience is equally important. AI tools like **TubeBuddy** and **VidIQ** offer SEO optimization features specifically for video platforms like YouTube. They can suggest keywords, analyze competitors, and even recommend optimal upload times based on audience behavior.

Tip for Content Creators: Use these tools to optimize not only your video titles and descriptions but also your tags and thumbnails. Effective use of metadata can significantly increase your video's discoverability.

Exercise:

1. Upload a video to your YouTube channel.
2. Use TubeBuddy to analyze your current tags and identify opportunities for optimization.
3. Update your video's metadata based on these insights and monitor its performance over the next few weeks.

2. AI for Social Media Video Optimization

Social media platforms like Instagram and TikTok have their own sets of requirements and best practices. Tools like **Kapwing** and **InVideo** offer templates and editing features optimized for different platforms, ensuring your content looks professional and performs well across various social channels.

Practical Use Case: You've created a long-form YouTube video and now want to repurpose it for Instagram Reels. Instead of manually editing and reformatting, use Kapwing to quickly generate a vertical, 15-second version with the most impactful highlights, complete with captions and effects.

Exercise:

1. Choose a 60-second segment from one of your existing videos.
2. Use Kapwing to reformat it for TikTok or Instagram Reels, adding captions and stickers to enhance engagement.
3. Post the reformatted video and track its performance compared to the original.

Case Studies: AI in Video Editing

Case Study 1: Automating Social Media Content for a Fashion Brand

A mid-sized fashion brand wanted to increase their social media presence but found it difficult to keep up with the demands of regular video content. They turned to **Lumen5**, an AI video creation platform that transforms blog posts into engaging videos. By using Lumen5, they were able to generate short, visually appealing videos highlighting key trends and fashion tips directly from their existing blog content. This not only increased their video output but also boosted their engagement on Instagram and Facebook by 35%.

Takeaway: AI tools like Lumen5 can help repurpose existing content into new formats, saving time and resources while reaching a broader audience.

Case Study 2: Creating Personalized Marketing Videos at Scale

A SaaS company used **Synthesia**, an AI video generation tool, to create personalized videos for each of their top 500 clients. The videos featured a virtual spokesperson addressing each client by name, discussing specific product features relevant to their business needs. The personalized approach resulted in a 60% increase in open rates and a 40% boost in product demo bookings compared to standard email marketing campaigns.

Takeaway: Personalization can significantly enhance engagement. AI video tools make it feasible to create customized content at scale, even for smaller teams.

Overcoming Challenges in AI Video Editing

1. Maintaining Human Touch in AI-Edited Videos

AI tools can sometimes produce videos that feel formulaic or lack emotional depth. To avoid this, always review and refine AI-edited content, adding personal touches such as voiceovers, unique transitions, or custom animations.

Exercise:

1. Create a video using an AI editing tool like Magisto.
2. Watch the video and identify any sections that feel too generic or automated.
3. Re-edit those sections manually, adding personal elements like voice narration or personalized text overlays.

2. Balancing Efficiency with Creativity

While AI tools can automate many aspects of video editing, it's essential to maintain a balance between efficiency and creativity. Use AI for repetitive tasks, but ensure that the final cut reflects your creative vision and storytelling style.

Exercise:

1. Choose a simple project and let an AI tool handle the initial edit.
2. Watch the AI-edited video and note any areas that don't align with your vision.
3. Make manual adjustments, focusing on elements like pacing, music choice, and visual style.

Conclusion: Embracing AI as a Creative Partner

AI is transforming the world of video editing, making it more accessible and efficient for creators at all levels. By integrating AI tools into your workflow, you can produce high-quality video content faster and with greater ease. Remember, AI is not here to replace your creativity but to enhance it, allowing you to focus on what truly matters: telling compelling stories that resonate with your audience.

In the next chapter, we'll delve into AI tools for graphic design, exploring how they can help creators produce stunning visuals, streamline design workflows, and unlock new creative possibilities.

Chapter 4: AI for Graphic Design

Introduction: Enhancing Creativity and Efficiency in Graphic Design

Graphic design is a blend of creativity, technical skill, and a keen eye for aesthetics. Whether you're designing logos, social media graphics, or complex digital illustrations, the process often involves repetitive tasks and intricate details. AI is revolutionizing this space by automating mundane tasks, generating creative assets, and providing powerful tools for visual experimentation. In this chapter, we'll explore how AI can enhance the graphic design process, from ideation and layout to final touches and optimization.

AI Tools for Graphic Design: Transforming the Creative Process

AI tools are not just for data scientists or developers—they're becoming essential for designers too. These tools help automate tasks like background removal, color correction, and even design creation, allowing designers to focus more on the creative aspects of their work.

1. Canva and Adobe Spark: Simplifying Design for Everyone

Platforms like **Canva** and **Adobe Spark** have democratized graphic design by offering easy-to-use interfaces combined with powerful AI features. Canva's **Magic Resize** tool, for instance, allows designers to quickly adapt a single design for multiple platforms, saving hours of manual resizing and layout adjustments.

Practical Example: Suppose you've created a promotional graphic for a new product launch. With Canva's Magic Resize, you can instantly generate versions optimized for Instagram, Facebook, and email headers, ensuring a consistent look across all platforms.

Exercise:

1. Create a simple promotional graphic in Canva.
2. Use the Magic Resize tool to adapt the design for different social media platforms.
3. Adjust each version to ensure the text and images are appropriately scaled and positioned.

Automated Design Generation: Exploring New Possibilities

1. Design Generators like Designify and Looka

Design generators are powerful tools that can create logos, business cards, and even entire brand identities with just a few inputs. **Designify**, for example, uses AI to enhance and stylize photos, making it easy to create eye-catching visuals with minimal effort. Meanwhile, **Looka** specializes in logo creation, using AI to generate hundreds of logo variations based on your brand name and industry.

Practical Use Case: A startup founder with no design background needs a professional logo for their new app. By using Looka, they can input their app name and industry, and within minutes, they have several polished logo designs to choose from. They can then customize colors, fonts, and layouts to match their vision.

Exercise:

1. Use Looka to generate a logo for a fictional brand.
2. Experiment with different color schemes and fonts to see how each change affects the brand's identity.
3. Download the final version and create a mockup for business cards or social media headers.

2. DALL-E and MidJourney: AI-Generated Artwork

For more experimental or artistic projects, AI tools like **DALL-E** and **MidJourney** can generate unique visuals from text prompts. These tools allow designers to create surreal, abstract, or highly detailed artwork that might be difficult or time-consuming to produce manually.

Practical Example: You're working on a digital illustration for a sci-fi book cover. By inputting a prompt like "futuristic cityscape under a starry sky," DALL-E can generate multiple interpretations of this scene, providing inspiration and a starting point for your design.

Exercise:

1. Use DALL-E or MidJourney to generate artwork based on a creative prompt of your choice.
2. Choose your favorite generated image and use it as a base for a more detailed illustration in software like Adobe Illustrator or Procreate.
3. Refine and add your own elements to the image to create a cohesive final piece.

Automating Repetitive Tasks in Graphic Design

1. Background Removal and Image Enhancement

One of the most time-consuming aspects of graphic design is isolating subjects from backgrounds. Tools like **Remove.bg** and **Adobe Photoshop's AI-powered Select Subject** can handle this task with remarkable precision, allowing designers to focus on more complex editing and compositional work.

Tip for Designers: Use AI tools for initial background removal and then manually refine the selection edges to achieve a professional, polished look.

Exercise:

1. Select a high-quality image with a clear subject (e.g., a portrait or product photo).
2. Use Remove.bg to remove the background and download the isolated subject.
3. Open the image in Adobe Photoshop and refine the edges using the Refine Edge tool to ensure a clean cutout.

2. Colorization and Restoration of Old Photos

AI tools are also being used to breathe new life into old photographs. Platforms like **DeOldify** and **Colourise.sg** use machine learning to add color to black-and-white photos, restore faded colors, and enhance image quality.

Practical Example: A family historian uses DeOldify to colorize old family photos for a digital scrapbook. The AI-generated colors bring new life to these images, making them more engaging and relatable for younger generations.

Exercise:

1. Choose an old black-and-white photo from a public domain source.
2. Use DeOldify to add color to the image.
3. Adjust the colors manually in a photo editing tool like GIMP or Photoshop to enhance details and correct any inaccuracies.

AI in Typography and Layout Design

1. Automated Typography with Fontjoy and Google Fonts AI

Choosing the right font combinations can be a challenging and time-consuming process. Tools like **Fontjoy** use AI to suggest harmonious font pairings based on visual contrast, style, and readability. Google Fonts also offers an AI-powered feature that suggests font pairings and displays them in sample layouts, helping designers visualize their choices in real-world applications.

Practical Use Case: A web designer is creating a landing page for a tech startup. Using Fontjoy, they experiment with different font pairings until they find a combination that reflects the modern, innovative spirit of the brand.

Exercise:

1. Go to Fontjoy and select a primary font for a mock website header.
2. Experiment with different secondary fonts for body text and call-to-action buttons.
3. Implement these font choices in a website mockup using a tool like Figma or Adobe XD.

2. AI-Driven Layout Design with Canva's Smart Design and Adobe Sensei

Layout design involves placing text, images, and other elements in a way that is both aesthetically pleasing and functional. Canva's **Smart Design** feature automatically suggests layout options based on the elements you've added, while **Adobe Sensei** offers intelligent cropping and content-aware layout suggestions in Adobe InDesign.

Practical Example: A freelance designer is creating a multi-page brochure. By using Adobe Sensei, they can quickly adjust the layout of each page, ensuring that images and text flow naturally without manually resizing or repositioning elements.

Exercise:

1. Create a basic layout for a two-page brochure in Adobe InDesign.

2. Use Adobe Sensei's content-aware features to experiment with different layout options.
3. Adjust the final layout based on these suggestions, adding your own design elements and style.

Case Studies: AI in Graphic Design

Case Study 1: Revamping Brand Identity with AI Tools

A small e-commerce business wanted to update its brand identity to reflect its growing audience and evolving product line. Using Looka, they generated a new logo that was modern and professional. They then used Canva to create a series of marketing materials, including social media templates and business cards. The rebranding effort resulted in a 50% increase in brand recognition and a 30% boost in social media engagement.

Takeaway: AI tools can empower businesses, even those without in-house design teams, to create cohesive and professional brand identities.

Case Study 2: Streamlining Creative Workflows for a Design Agency

A design agency integrated AI tools like Remove.bg and Adobe Sensei into their workflow to handle repetitive tasks such as background removal and layout adjustments. This allowed their designers to focus more on creative brainstorming and client interactions. As a result, the agency was able to increase their project throughput by 20%, leading to higher client satisfaction and more repeat business.

Takeaway: AI can significantly streamline workflows, allowing designers to allocate more time to the creative and strategic aspects of their projects.

Overcoming Challenges in AI Graphic Design

1. Balancing AI Assistance with Creative Control

While AI can handle many technical tasks, it's important to maintain creative control over your work. AI-generated designs can sometimes feel generic or lack the personal touch that makes great design stand out. Use AI tools to automate routine tasks, but always add your unique flair and creativity to the final design.

Exercise:

1. Use an AI design tool to create a basic layout or template for a project.
2. Customize the template extensively, adding unique elements, adjusting colors, and experimenting with different compositions.
3. Compare the AI-generated template with your customized version and reflect on the improvements.

2. Avoiding Over-Reliance on AI

It's easy to become overly reliant on AI tools, especially when they make tasks so much faster and easier. However, relying too much on AI can limit your growth as a designer. Make sure to continue developing your manual design skills and use AI as a tool to enhance your capabilities, not replace them.

Exercise:

1. Choose a design project that you would typically do with AI assistance.
2. Complete the project manually, focusing on developing your skills in areas like typography, color theory, and layout design.
3. After completing the manual version, compare it to a version created with AI and analyze the differences.

Conclusion: Embracing AI as a Tool for Innovation

AI is transforming graphic design, offering powerful tools that enhance creativity, streamline workflows, and make high-quality design accessible to everyone. By integrating AI into your design process, you can produce stunning visuals more efficiently while focusing on the artistic and strategic elements that truly define great design. Remember, AI is a tool to amplify your creativity, not to replace it. Use it wisely to push the boundaries of what's possible in your work.

In the next chapter, we'll explore how AI can optimize social media content creation, from generating posts to scheduling and analytics. Get ready to take your social media strategy to the next level!

Chapter 5: AI in Social Media Content Creation

Introduction: The Power of AI in Social Media Marketing

Social media has become a cornerstone of digital marketing, allowing brands and creators to engage directly with their audiences. However, maintaining a consistent and engaging presence across multiple platforms can be challenging and time-consuming. AI is changing the game by automating various aspects of social media content creation, from planning and generating posts to optimizing engagement and scheduling. In this chapter, we'll explore how AI can help you create compelling social media content that resonates with your audience and enhances your digital presence.

AI-Powered Tools for Social Media Content Creation

AI tools are revolutionizing how we create and manage social media content. They help generate ideas, write posts, design visuals, and even analyze performance—all essential for a successful social media strategy.

1. AI for Content Ideation and Generation

Coming up with fresh content ideas and writing engaging posts are often the most daunting parts of managing social media. AI tools like **Copy.ai** and **Writesonic** can generate post ideas, captions, and even entire blog articles based on a few keywords or a brief prompt.

Practical Example: You're running a social media campaign for a new product launch. After inputting a few details about the product into Copy.ai, it generates a series of social media posts, including promotional captions, engaging questions, and even a mini-blog post summarizing the product's benefits. This gives you a solid foundation to build on, saving time and ensuring your messaging is consistent across platforms.

Exercise:

1. Choose a product or service you want to promote.
2. Use Copy.ai or Writesonic to generate five different social media posts.
3. Edit and personalize these posts to align with your brand voice and style.

2. Visual Content Creation with AI

Visuals are crucial for grabbing attention on social media. AI tools like **Canva** and **Crello** offer a range of templates, while more advanced platforms like **Designify** and **DeepArt.io** can create unique visuals based on text inputs or existing images. These tools are particularly useful for creating eye-catching graphics for posts, stories, and ads.

Practical Use Case: Imagine you're preparing a series of Instagram posts for a seasonal sale. You can use Canva's AI-powered design features to create cohesive visuals for each post, complete with customized fonts, colors, and imagery that reflect the sale's theme.

Exercise:

1. Choose a theme for a social media campaign (e.g., holiday sale).
2. Use Canva to create a set of three cohesive visuals, such as a promotional post, a countdown story, and an announcement post.
3. Ensure each design follows your brand guidelines and includes engaging call-to-action elements.

Automating Social Media Planning and Scheduling

1. Content Planning and Calendar Management

Planning content in advance is key to maintaining a consistent social media presence. Tools like **Buffer** and **Planoly** allow you to create and manage content calendars, providing a visual overview of scheduled posts across different platforms. AI-powered features, such as best-time-to-post suggestions, help ensure your content reaches the maximum number of people.

Tip for Social Media Managers: Use AI tools to analyze your audience's behavior and adjust your posting schedule accordingly. This can significantly boost engagement and interaction with your posts.

Exercise:

1. Use a tool like Planoly to create a content calendar for the next month.
2. Schedule posts at different times and analyze engagement metrics to determine the optimal posting times for your audience.
3. Adjust your future content calendar based on these insights.

2. Automated Posting and Engagement

Once your content is planned, tools like **Hootsuite** and **Later** can handle the scheduling and posting, allowing you to focus on engaging with your audience. Some AI-driven platforms, like **SocialBee**, even offer automated engagement features that can help respond to comments and messages, ensuring you stay connected with your followers without being tied to your phone 24/7.

Practical Use Case: A small business owner uses SocialBee to automate responses to frequently asked questions on Instagram.

This allows them to focus on running their business while still maintaining a strong social media presence.

Exercise:

1. Choose a series of posts you want to automate.
2. Use Hootsuite or Later to schedule these posts, adding hashtags and location tags as appropriate.
3. Set up automated responses for common queries using SocialBee or a similar tool.

AI for Optimizing Engagement and Performance

1. AI-Driven Analytics and Insights

Understanding what works and what doesn't is crucial for refining your social media strategy. AI-powered analytics tools like **Sprout Social** and **Iconosquare** can provide detailed insights into your content's performance, including engagement rates, audience demographics, and optimal posting times.

Practical Example: You've noticed a dip in engagement on your recent posts. Using Sprout Social, you discover that posts with more visual content (such as infographics and videos) perform significantly better than text-based posts. You adjust your strategy to include more visuals and see a 25% increase in engagement over the next month.

Exercise:

1. Use an analytics tool like Sprout Social to review the performance of your recent social media posts.
2. Identify the top-performing posts and analyze what made them successful (e.g., type of content, time of posting, captions).

3. Use these insights to create a revised content plan for the next month, incorporating similar elements.

2. AI for Social Listening and Trend Analysis

Keeping up with trends and understanding what your audience is talking about is vital for creating relevant content. AI tools like **Brandwatch** and **Awario** help track mentions, hashtags, and keywords across social platforms, giving you a real-time view of trending topics and audience sentiment.

Practical Use Case: A beauty brand uses Brandwatch to monitor social media conversations about skincare trends. They notice a spike in discussions about "blue light protection" and quickly create a series of posts highlighting their products that offer this benefit. The timely content resonates with their audience, leading to a significant increase in engagement and product inquiries.

Exercise:

1. Choose a keyword or hashtag relevant to your brand or industry.
2. Use a tool like Brandwatch to track mentions and analyze trends over the past month.
3. Create a piece of social media content (e.g., a post, infographic, or video) based on these insights and monitor its performance.

Enhancing Social Media Strategies with AI

1. AI for Influencer Marketing

Finding and collaborating with the right influencers can significantly amplify your reach. AI platforms like **Influencity** and **Upfluence** analyze millions of social media profiles to help identify influencers whose audience aligns with your brand. These tools provide detailed analytics on follower demographics, engagement rates, and content performance, ensuring you partner with the best fit.

Practical Example: A fitness brand is looking to promote a new line of protein supplements. Using Influencity, they identify a group of micro-influencers with strong engagement in the health and fitness community. By collaborating on a series of workout and nutrition posts, the brand reaches a highly targeted audience and sees a boost in product sales.

Exercise:

1. Use a tool like Influencity to find potential influencers in your niche.
2. Analyze their profiles to assess their alignment with your brand (e.g., engagement rates, follower demographics).
3. Develop a collaboration proposal, including content ideas and campaign goals.

2. Generating Hashtags and Captions with AI

Choosing the right hashtags and crafting engaging captions can significantly boost your content's visibility and engagement. AI tools like **RiteTag** and **Captiona** suggest trending hashtags and caption ideas based on your content, helping you optimize your posts for maximum reach.

Practical Use Case: A travel blogger is preparing a post about a recent trip to Iceland. Using RiteTag, they generate a list of high-performing hashtags like #IcelandTravel and #Wanderlust, ensuring their post reaches a broader audience interested in travel content.

Exercise:

1. Write a draft caption for a social media post.
2. Use Captiona to generate alternative captions and RiteTag to find relevant hashtags.

3. Compare the generated suggestions and choose the best ones to optimize your post.

Case Studies: AI in Social Media Content Creation

Case Study 1: Scaling Social Media Presence for a Startup

A tech startup wanted to increase its social media presence but had a limited team and budget. By using Copy.ai for content generation and Buffer for scheduling, they were able to plan and post regularly without overwhelming their small team. This consistent presence led to a 300% increase in followers and a 150% increase in website traffic from social channels within six months.

Takeaway: AI tools can help small teams maintain a strong social media presence without requiring extensive resources.

Case Study 2: Boosting Engagement with AI-Optimized Content

A fashion brand noticed that their Instagram engagement had plateaued. They used Iconosquare to analyze their content and discovered that posts featuring behind-the-scenes videos and user-generated content performed best. By shifting their strategy to focus on these types of posts, they saw a 45% increase in engagement over three months.

Takeaway: Regularly analyzing performance data and adjusting your strategy based on AI-driven insights can significantly improve engagement and reach.

Overcoming Challenges in AI-Driven Social Media

1. Avoiding Content Homogeneity

While AI can generate a lot of content quickly, it can sometimes lead to posts that feel repetitive or generic. To keep your social media feed fresh and engaging, use AI for initial drafts and ideas but infuse them with your unique brand voice and creativity.

Exercise:

1. Use an AI tool to generate a series of social media posts on a specific topic.
2. Personalize each post with unique elements such as personal anecdotes, specific questions, or brand-specific language.
3. Compare the original AI-generated posts with your final versions and note the improvements.

2. Balancing Automation and Authentic Engagement

While automated responses and scheduling can save time, it's important to maintain authentic interactions with your audience. Make sure to regularly check your accounts and personally respond to comments and messages that require a more human touch.

Exercise:

1. Review your automated responses and adjust them to sound more conversational and authentic.
2. Set aside time each day to manually engage with your audience, responding to comments, messages, and mentions.

Conclusion: Leveraging AI for Social Media Success

AI tools are transforming how we create, manage, and optimize social media content. By integrating these technologies into your workflow, you can save time, increase engagement, and ensure that your social media strategy is both effective and scalable. However, it's crucial to use AI as a complement to, not a replacement for, genuine human creativity and interaction. With the right balance, you can elevate your social media presence and connect more deeply with your audience.

Chapter 6: Collaborative AI Tools for Teams

Introduction: Enhancing Team Collaboration with AI

Content creation is rarely a solo endeavor. Whether you're working within a marketing department, a design agency, or a distributed team of freelancers, effective collaboration is essential for producing high-quality work on time. AI-powered collaborative tools are transforming how teams create, share, and refine content. These tools help streamline project management, facilitate real-time editing, and even assist with creative brainstorming. In this chapter, we'll explore the best AI tools for team collaboration and how they can be integrated into your workflows to boost productivity and creativity.

AI Tools for Real-Time Collaboration and Project Management

Managing a team of content creators involves coordinating various tasks, deadlines, and feedback loops. AI-driven project management tools help organize these elements seamlessly, making it easier for teams to stay on track and collaborate effectively.

1. Trello and Asana: Smart Task Management

While Trello and Asana are well-known project management tools, their AI-powered features take collaboration to the next level. For example, Asana's AI can predict project delays by analyzing patterns in task completion and dependencies, alerting teams before potential bottlenecks occur. Trello's **Butler** automation tool uses machine learning to suggest workflow improvements, automate repetitive tasks, and ensure nothing falls through the cracks.

Practical Use Case: A content team is planning a large-scale product launch campaign. By using Asana's AI features, they can track the progress of each content piece, from ideation to publication, and receive notifications if any deadlines are at risk of being missed.

Exercise:

1. Set up a project in Asana with multiple tasks, dependencies, and deadlines.
2. Use the predictive analysis feature to identify any potential delays and reassign tasks as needed to keep the project on track.
3. Implement Trello's Butler automation to streamline repetitive processes, such as assigning labels or moving cards based on task completion.

2. Notion and ClickUp: Centralized Knowledge Management

Centralizing team knowledge and resources is critical for efficient collaboration. Tools like **Notion** and **ClickUp** integrate AI to enhance search capabilities, automate workflows, and even suggest relevant resources or templates based on project needs. Notion's AI-powered database search can quickly surface relevant documents, saving time otherwise spent digging through files.

Practical Example: A digital agency uses Notion to store client briefs, style guides, and project templates. With AI-enhanced search, team members can quickly find relevant information, such as client preferences or brand guidelines, without sifting through multiple folders.

Exercise:

1. Create a knowledge base in Notion, including sections for client information, style guides, and project templates.
2. Use AI search to find specific information (e.g., "social media guidelines" or "approved fonts") and test its accuracy and speed.
3. Set up automated workflows in ClickUp, such as task creation from meeting notes or client emails, to streamline project setup.

AI for Creative Collaboration and Brainstorming

Creativity thrives on collaboration, and AI can enhance brainstorming sessions by generating ideas, offering content suggestions, and even facilitating creative workshops.

1. Miro and Stormboard: AI for Virtual Brainstorming

Virtual whiteboard tools like **Miro** and **Stormboard** are essential for remote teams, allowing them to collaborate on ideas in real time. AI features in these tools can help organize brainstorming sessions, suggest ideas based on keywords, and even prioritize concepts based on their potential impact.

Practical Use Case: A marketing team is planning a new campaign. During a virtual brainstorming session on Miro, they use the AI-powered sticky notes feature to generate and categorize ideas. The AI then suggests related concepts and even flags the most promising ideas for further exploration.

Exercise:

1. Set up a brainstorming session in Miro or Stormboard focused on a specific project, like developing a new content series.
2. Use AI tools to generate additional ideas based on your team's inputs.
3. Categorize and prioritize the ideas using AI suggestions, then create a plan to develop the top concepts.

2. Sudowrite and Jasper: AI for Collaborative Writing

Collaborative writing can be challenging, especially when multiple team members contribute to the same document. AI tools like **Sudowrite** and **Jasper** facilitate this process by suggesting content additions, providing real-time feedback, and even rephrasing text to ensure a consistent tone and style.

Practical Example: A content team is co-writing a series of blog posts. Using Sudowrite, they can collaboratively generate ideas, get AI-powered feedback on structure and flow, and ensure that the posts maintain a unified voice, regardless of the number of contributors.

Exercise:

1. Choose a topic for a blog post and set up a shared document in Google Docs.
2. Use Sudowrite to generate an outline collaboratively, then have each team member add their own sections.
3. Review the document using Jasper's AI suggestions to refine the text and ensure a consistent style throughout.

AI for Streamlining Feedback and Approval Workflows

Providing feedback and managing approvals can be cumbersome, particularly for larger teams. AI tools streamline these processes, ensuring that feedback is clear, constructive, and easily incorporated into revisions.

1. Filestage and Frame.io: AI for Media Review and Approval

For teams working with visual or video content, tools like **Filestage** and **Frame.io** offer AI-powered annotation and version tracking. These platforms allow team members to leave time-stamped comments, highlight specific areas of a design or video, and even suggest edits directly within the file. AI can then compile these comments into actionable to-do lists, making the revision process smoother.

Practical Use Case: A video production team is finalizing an advertisement. Using Frame.io, team members leave feedback on specific scenes, and the AI aggregates these comments, creating a task list for the editor to address. This reduces the back-and-forth typically associated with video revisions.

Exercise:

1. Upload a video or design file to Frame.io or Filestage.
2. Leave feedback on different elements, such as timing, transitions, or visual effects.
3. Use the AI-generated to-do list to make the suggested edits, ensuring all feedback is incorporated before final approval.

2. Zoho Writer and Grammarly Business: AI for Document Review

When multiple stakeholders need to review and approve written content, tools like **Zoho Writer** and **Grammarly Business** can help. Zoho Writer's AI features can automatically suggest changes based on internal style guides, while Grammarly Business provides advanced grammar and clarity suggestions, ensuring that content is polished and professional.

Practical Example: An editorial team is preparing a white paper that needs approval from various departments. Using Zoho Writer, they set up an AI-driven workflow that suggests edits based on the company's style guide and automatically notifies the next reviewer when their input is needed.

Exercise:

1. Draft a document in Zoho Writer and share it with your team.
2. Set up an AI-driven approval workflow, assigning different team members to review and approve specific sections.
3. Use Grammarly Business to refine the document, incorporating any additional suggestions before final approval.

Enhancing Communication and Collaboration with AI

Effective communication is crucial for successful collaboration, especially in distributed or remote teams. AI tools can help bridge communication gaps, ensure clarity, and keep everyone on the same page.

1. Slack and Microsoft Teams: AI for Enhanced Communication

Platforms like **Slack** and **Microsoft Teams** integrate AI to improve communication through features like automated reminders, meeting summaries, and intelligent search. AI can even detect when a conversation needs escalation (e.g., a project delay) and automatically create a task or reminder to address it.

Practical Use Case: During a busy week, a project manager might miss some important messages in Slack. Using AI-powered reminders, Slack automatically flags messages related to urgent tasks and creates a summary of key points, ensuring that nothing critical is overlooked.

Exercise:

1. Set up a project-specific channel in Slack or Microsoft Teams.
2. Use AI-powered features to create automated reminders for upcoming deadlines and meetings.
3. Enable intelligent search to quickly find past discussions and decisions related to your project.

2. Crystal and Otter.ai: AI for Personalization and Meeting Summaries

AI tools like **Crystal** and **Otter.ai** offer unique ways to enhance communication. Crystal analyzes team members' communication styles and suggests personalized ways to interact with them, while Otter.ai transcribes meetings in real time, providing searchable summaries and action items.

Practical Example: A team lead wants to improve communication with a new member who prefers concise, data-driven updates. Using Crystal, the lead tailors their communication style to match the new member's preferences, improving collaboration and productivity. Meanwhile, Otter.ai transcribes their meetings, allowing everyone to focus on the discussion instead of taking notes.

Exercise:

1. Use Crystal to analyze your communication style and compare it with a team member's style.
2. Adjust your next email or message to this team member based on Crystal's suggestions.
3. Record your next meeting with Otter.ai and use the transcription to create a summary and list of action items.

Case Studies: AI for Collaborative Content Creation

Case Study 1: Streamlining Content Production for a Global Marketing Team

A global marketing team faced challenges coordinating content production across multiple time zones. They implemented a combination of Notion for knowledge management, Asana for project tracking, and Slack for communication. Using AI features like automated task assignments and intelligent document search, they reduced project turnaround times by 30% and improved cross-team collaboration.

Takeaway: Integrating AI tools across project management, knowledge sharing, and communication platforms can significantly improve collaboration and efficiency, especially for distributed teams.

Case Study 2: Improving Creative Collaboration in a Design Agency

A design agency used Miro for virtual brainstorming and Frame.io for video review. The AI features in these tools helped organize ideas, prioritize feedback, and streamline the revision process. As a result, the agency was able to handle a 20% increase in projects without adding new staff, while maintaining high-quality output and client satisfaction.

Takeaway: AI-powered creative tools can enhance collaboration and productivity, enabling teams to manage more projects and deliver higher-quality work.

Overcoming Challenges in AI-Powered Team Collaboration

1. Maintaining Human Touch in AI-Driven Collaboration

While AI can automate many aspects of collaboration, it's important to maintain a human touch. AI-generated suggestions can sometimes feel impersonal or overly rigid. Encourage team members to use AI tools as a guide, but to add their own insights and creativity to the process.

Exercise:

1. Use an AI tool to generate an initial project outline or plan.
2. Discuss the AI-generated plan with your team, gathering feedback and suggestions for improvement.
3. Adjust the plan based on team input, ensuring it reflects both AI insights and human perspectives.

2. Balancing Automation and Engagement

AI can handle repetitive tasks, but too much automation can lead to disengagement. Make sure to balance automated workflows with opportunities for meaningful human interaction, such as brainstorming sessions, team check-ins, and collaborative workshops.

Exercise:

1. Identify tasks in your workflow that are heavily automated (e.g., project updates, meeting scheduling).
2. Schedule regular team check-ins or creative workshops to complement these automated processes and keep team members engaged and aligned.
3. Use feedback from these sessions to adjust your workflows, ensuring they support both efficiency and team collaboration.

Conclusion: AI as a Catalyst for Team Collaboration

AI tools are transforming how teams collaborate, offering new ways to streamline workflows, enhance creativity, and improve communication. By integrating these technologies into your team's processes, you can boost productivity and create a more cohesive, efficient, and creative work environment. Remember, AI is a tool to support and enhance human collaboration, not to replace it. Use it thoughtfully to empower your team and elevate your collaborative efforts.

Chapter 7: Overcoming Challenges in AI Content Creation

Introduction: Navigating the Complexities of AI-Assisted Creativity

While AI offers numerous advantages in content creation, it's not without its challenges. From maintaining a unique voice to addressing ethical concerns, content creators must navigate a complex landscape when integrating AI into their workflows. This chapter will explore common challenges faced by creators and provide strategies to overcome them. We'll also look ahead to potential future developments in AI that could further revolutionize the creative process, from advanced AI-driven personalization to fully autonomous content creation systems.

Challenge 1: Maintaining Authenticity and Creativity

One of the primary concerns for creators using AI is the potential loss of authenticity and creativity. AI tools can generate content quickly, but they often lack the emotional depth and unique voice that make creative work compelling. Many creators worry that their work will become formulaic or indistinguishable from machine-generated content.

Strategies for Preserving Authenticity

1. **Blend AI and Human Input**: Use AI as a starting point for drafts, ideas, or outlines, but always refine and expand the content with your unique perspective. For example, a writer can use tools like **Sudowrite** to generate plot twists or dialogue for a story but should edit and personalize these elements to ensure they align with their creative vision.
2. **Set Boundaries for AI Use**: Define specific roles for AI tools within your creative process. For instance, use AI for ideation and technical tasks like grammar checking, but

reserve creative decision-making, tone, and style adjustments for yourself.
3. **Use AI to Enhance, Not Replace**: Instead of relying solely on AI-generated content, use these tools to enhance your work. For example, an illustrator might use AI-generated textures or patterns as a base, then build on them with traditional techniques to create unique, hybrid artworks.

Future Possibility: **AI Co-Creation Systems** Imagine AI tools that can collaborate with you in real time, adjusting content based on your feedback. These systems would not just generate text or visuals but would engage in a dialogue, learning your style and preferences over time. For example, a writer's AI assistant could suggest edits in a specific voice or narrative style, while a visual artist's AI could offer design elements that match their aesthetic.

Challenge 2: Managing Bias and Ethical Concerns

AI systems are trained on existing data, which can introduce biases and ethical issues into the content they generate. This can result in unintended stereotypes, biased language, or unbalanced representations, particularly in creative fields like writing, art, and media.

Strategies for Ethical AI Use

1. **Audit AI Outputs Regularly**: Regularly review AI-generated content for potential biases or ethical issues. Tools like **Hugging Face's Model Card Toolkit** can help creators understand the limitations and biases of the AI models they use.
2. **Diversify Training Data**: For creators building custom AI models, using diverse and representative training data can help mitigate bias. This approach ensures that the AI generates content that is inclusive and balanced.
3. **Implement Ethical Guidelines**: Establish clear ethical guidelines for using AI in your creative work. This could include rules on how AI-generated content is labeled, how

human oversight is maintained, and how ethical concerns are addressed.

Future Possibility: **AI Ethics Protocols** Future AI systems could include built-in ethics protocols that automatically detect and flag biased or inappropriate content. These systems would analyze AI outputs against a set of ethical guidelines defined by the creator, helping to ensure that the content is aligned with the creator's values and social standards.

Challenge 3: Over-Reliance on AI Tools

As AI tools become more powerful and accessible, there's a risk of over-reliance. Creators may become dependent on AI for ideation and execution, which can stifle their own creativity and skill development.

Strategies to Avoid Over-Reliance

1. **Limit AI Usage**: Set limits on how and when you use AI tools. For example, dedicate specific time each week to work on projects without any AI assistance, focusing purely on your creative skills.
2. **Use AI for Inspiration, Not Substitution**: Instead of using AI to generate complete pieces, use it to inspire new ideas. For instance, a graphic designer might use an AI tool like **Deep Dream** to create abstract patterns, then incorporate these patterns into a larger, manually crafted design.
3. **Focus on Skill Development**: Continuously develop your skills independently of AI. Whether it's writing, drawing, or coding, maintaining and expanding your expertise ensures that you can use AI as a tool rather than a crutch.

Future Possibility: **AI-Assisted Skill Development** Imagine AI tools designed to help creators improve their skills through personalized feedback and training. These tools could analyze your work, identify areas for improvement, and provide targeted exercises or tutorials. For example, a writing assistant might suggest exercises to help strengthen your narrative pacing or dialogue skills, while a design assistant could offer tutorials on advanced illustration techniques.

Challenge 4: Integrating AI into Team Workflows

For teams, integrating AI into established workflows can be challenging. Team members may have different levels of familiarity and comfort with AI tools, and aligning everyone's use of these tools can be difficult.

Strategies for Effective AI Integration

1. **Provide Training and Resources**: Ensure that all team members have access to training and resources on how to use AI tools effectively. This can include workshops, tutorials, or even dedicated AI support within the team.
2. **Standardize AI Usage**: Develop a standard approach to using AI tools in your workflow. This includes defining which tools are used for specific tasks, how AI outputs are reviewed, and how human oversight is maintained.
3. **Encourage Collaboration Between AI and Human Creativity**: Promote collaborative projects where team members use AI to complement their skills. For example, a writer and an illustrator could use an AI tool like **Runway ML** to co-create a multimedia story, blending text and visuals in innovative ways.

Future Possibility: **AI Collaboration Platforms** Future collaboration platforms could offer integrated AI systems that adapt to each team member's role and preferences. These systems would facilitate seamless collaboration between human and AI contributors, allowing for dynamic content creation where AI assists in real time, suggesting edits, design elements, or even new creative directions based on the team's collective input.

Challenge 5: Keeping Up with Rapid AI Advancements

The pace of AI development is accelerating, with new tools and capabilities emerging constantly. This can make it difficult for creators to stay up-to-date and effectively integrate the latest advancements into their work.

Strategies for Staying Current

1. **Follow AI Trends and Communities**: Engage with AI and creative technology communities through platforms like GitHub, LinkedIn, or specialized forums. Following thought leaders and participating in discussions can help you stay informed about the latest developments.
2. **Experiment with New Tools Regularly**: Dedicate time to experimenting with new AI tools and features. This could be a monthly or quarterly activity where you test the latest software, assess its potential, and explore how it might fit into your creative process.
3. **Invest in Continuous Learning**: Take advantage of online courses, webinars, and workshops focused on AI and creative technology. This will not only keep you informed but also help you develop new skills and competencies that can expand your creative toolkit.

Future Possibility: **AI Discovery Platforms** Imagine an AI platform designed to keep creators up-to-date with the latest tools and technologies. This platform could curate a personalized feed of new AI tools, tutorials, and case studies based on your interests and creative projects, helping you discover and adopt innovations that align with your workflow.

Speculating on the Future: What's Next for AI in Content Creation?

As we look to the future, several exciting possibilities for AI in content creation are emerging. These advancements could further blur the lines between human and machine creativity, offering new opportunities and challenges for creators.

1. Fully Autonomous Content Creation Systems

Imagine a future where AI systems can generate entire content pieces autonomously, from ideation to execution. These systems could produce blog posts, videos, or even novels with minimal human input, adapting to different styles, tones, and formats. While this raises questions about the role of human creativity, it also offers new possibilities for content production at scale.

2. AI-Driven Personalization at Scale

Future AI systems could deliver hyper-personalized content experiences, tailoring not just recommendations but the content itself. For example, a news website could use AI to generate articles with different tones or emphases depending on the reader's preferences, or a streaming service could offer personalized versions of a film with different narrative paths based on viewer choices.

3. Integrated AI-Creator Workspaces

Imagine a fully integrated creative workspace where all your AI tools and creative assets are interconnected. In this environment, AI would not only assist with individual tasks but also provide real-time insights and suggestions across your entire creative process, from brainstorming and drafting to editing and publishing. This could include everything from automated resource management and intelligent asset tagging to collaborative AI agents that help coordinate team workflows.

Conclusion: Embracing the Future of AI-Enhanced Creativity

The challenges of integrating AI into content creation are real, but they are outweighed by the potential benefits. By understanding and addressing these challenges, creators can harness the power of AI to enhance their work, improve collaboration, and explore new creative possibilities. Looking forward, the future of AI in content creation is incredibly exciting, with innovations on the horizon that could transform how we create, share, and experience content.

Chapter 8: The Future of AI in Content Creation

Introduction: A New Era of Creative Potential

As we've explored throughout this book, AI is revolutionizing content creation in profound ways. From automating repetitive tasks to enabling new forms of creativity, AI tools have become invaluable partners for writers, designers, video editors, and social media managers. But this is just the beginning. As AI technology continues to advance, we are on the cusp of a new era where the boundaries between human and machine creativity will blur even further. In this final chapter, we'll speculate on the future of AI in content creation, explore emerging technologies, and provide strategies for staying ahead of the curve.

The Evolution of AI: From Assistive Tools to Creative Partners

The journey of AI in content creation has moved from simple automation to sophisticated assistance, and we're now entering an era where AI can actively collaborate with creators. This evolution raises exciting possibilities for the future:

1. Adaptive AI Systems

Imagine AI tools that not only understand your creative preferences but adapt to them over time. These adaptive systems would learn your style, preferences, and even your creative habits, providing more personalized and relevant suggestions as you work. For example, a writer's AI assistant could learn their preferred narrative structures and tone, suggesting plot developments and character arcs that align with their unique voice.

Future Vision: Adaptive AI could extend to visual arts and music, with tools that evolve alongside artists, offering brushstroke suggestions, color palettes, or musical arrangements tailored to their evolving style.

2. AI-Driven Multimodal Creativity

As AI systems become more sophisticated, we're likely to see greater integration across different forms of media. Imagine an AI that can seamlessly transition between writing, visual design, and video editing, creating cohesive multimedia content. For example, you could describe a story idea to an AI, which then generates a script, storyboard, visual elements, and even a short animated video—all in one integrated process.

Practical Application: A content creator could use this type of AI to develop a complete marketing campaign from a single concept, producing blog posts, social media graphics, and promotional videos with consistent messaging and aesthetics.

Exercise:

1. Write a brief story outline.
2. Use AI tools to generate a basic storyboard or visual representation of the scenes described.
3. Experiment with different media types, like text-to-video or image-to-music generators, to create a multimodal representation of your story.

Emerging Technologies: The Next Wave of AI Innovation

The future of AI in content creation will be shaped by several key technologies that are still in their early stages but hold immense potential.

1. Generative Adversarial Networks (GANs)

GANs have already shown their potential in creating realistic images, music, and even entire scenes for video games and films. In the future, GANs could be used to create highly detailed visual and audio content from simple prompts, enabling creators to generate complex, photorealistic environments or characters with minimal effort.

Future Possibility: Imagine a filmmaker using a GAN-based tool to generate virtual sets, complete with realistic lighting and textures, based on a few sketches or descriptions. This could dramatically reduce the cost and time of producing high-quality visual content.

2. Neural Storytellers and Narrative Engines

Advanced AI systems like OpenAI's GPT-4 have already shown their ability to generate coherent and engaging narratives. Future developments in neural storytelling could lead to AI systems that not only generate stories but also understand and manipulate complex narrative structures, themes, and emotional arcs.

Future Possibility: A game developer could use a narrative engine to generate dynamic storylines that adapt to player choices in real-time, creating a truly immersive and personalized gaming experience.

Exercise:

1. Develop a basic story idea and input it into a neural storytelling tool like Sudowrite or Narrative Device.
2. Experiment with different story paths and endings generated by the AI, then choose elements to refine and develop into a cohesive narrative.

3. AI-Enhanced Immersive Experiences

With advancements in augmented reality (AR) and virtual reality (VR), AI will play a crucial role in creating immersive digital experiences. Future AI systems could generate interactive environments and characters that respond to users in real time, enhancing everything from virtual storytelling to interactive art installations.

Future Vision: Imagine walking through a virtual art gallery where each painting changes in response to your gaze or gestures, or a VR story where characters react dynamically to your decisions and emotions, creating a deeply personalized narrative experience.

Exercise:

1. Create a simple VR or AR experience using tools like Unity or Spark AR.
2. Experiment with AI elements like interactive characters or responsive environments.
3. Explore how AI can enhance user engagement and create more immersive experiences.

The Future of Creative Collaboration: AI as a Team Member

As AI tools become more integrated and sophisticated, they will increasingly take on the role of active team members rather than just tools. Future AI systems could participate in brainstorming sessions, generate creative content suggestions, and even provide feedback in real time, helping teams collaborate more effectively across disciplines and time zones.

Example: A remote design team could work with an AI system that generates visual concepts based on verbal descriptions during a video call. The team could then refine these concepts together in real time, with the AI adjusting its outputs based on the team's feedback.

Exercise:

1. Conduct a brainstorming session with your team using a collaborative AI tool like Miro or Stormboard.
2. Input initial ideas and use the AI to generate additional suggestions and refine the concepts.

3. Develop a project plan based on the AI-augmented brainstorming session, assigning roles and tasks to each team member.

Preparing for the Future: Strategies for Staying Ahead

With so many exciting developments on the horizon, it's crucial for content creators to stay proactive and adaptable. Here are some strategies to ensure you remain at the forefront of the AI-driven creative revolution:

1. Continuously Experiment with New Tools

The AI landscape is evolving rapidly, with new tools and capabilities emerging all the time. Dedicate regular time to exploring and experimenting with new technologies, even if they're outside your current expertise. This could involve attending workshops, participating in beta testing, or simply setting aside a few hours each month to explore new tools and platforms.

Practical Tip: Follow AI and creative technology newsletters, forums, and social media channels to stay informed about the latest innovations and trends.

2. Invest in Cross-Disciplinary Skills

As AI tools enable more integrated and multimodal content creation, having a diverse skill set will become increasingly valuable. Consider learning complementary skills such as coding, design, or video production to expand your creative capabilities and make the most of AI's potential.

Exercise:

1. Choose a new skill that complements your primary creative focus (e.g., learning basic Python for automation or mastering Adobe Premiere for video editing).

2. Dedicate a set amount of time each week to developing this skill.
3. Apply your new knowledge to a small project, incorporating AI tools to enhance your workflow.

3. Collaborate with AI Enthusiasts and Experts

Networking with others who are passionate about AI can provide valuable insights, inspiration, and collaboration opportunities. Engage with communities of AI enthusiasts, developers, and creators to exchange ideas and explore new ways to integrate AI into your work.

Practical Tip: Join online communities like AI-focused LinkedIn groups, Reddit forums, or Discord channels where you can discuss the latest advancements, share projects, and collaborate on new ideas.

Embracing the Future: The Role of Human Creativity

As AI continues to evolve, it's natural to wonder about the role of human creativity in an increasingly automated world. The answer lies in collaboration. AI can generate, assist, and even inspire, but it is the human touch that brings depth, nuance, and emotional resonance to creative work. The future of content creation will not be a question of human versus machine, but rather how we can use these powerful new tools to amplify our creative potential and tell stories that resonate more deeply with our audiences.

Final Thoughts: The Creative Frontier

We are standing at the edge of a new creative frontier. AI is not just a tool; it is a catalyst for innovation, challenging us to rethink how we create, collaborate, and connect. As we move forward, the most successful creators will be those who embrace AI as a partner in their creative journey, using it to explore new possibilities, push boundaries, and create content that inspires and engages.

Remember, the future is not just something that happens to us—it is something we shape through our actions and choices. So, embrace the tools and technologies at your disposal, keep learning and experimenting, and never stop exploring the limitless potential of your creativity.

Thank you for joining us on this journey through the evolving world of AI in content creation. We hope this book has inspired you to harness the power of AI to elevate your creative work and explore new frontiers in your craft. The future of creativity is bright, and it's just beginning.

Here is the list of all the unique tools discussed:-

Adobe Spark - https://spark.adobe.com
Asana - https://asana.com
Awario - https://awario.com
Brandwatch - https://www.brandwatch.com
Buffer - https://buffer.com
BuzzSumo - https://buzzsumo.com
Canva - https://www.canva.com
Captiona - https://captiona.com
ClickUp - https://clickup.com
Content Samurai (Vidnami) - https://www.vidnami.com
Copy.ai - https://www.copy.ai
Crystal - https://www.crystalknows.com
DALL-E - https://openai.com/dall-e
DeepArt.io - https://deepart.io
Designify - https://www.designify.com
Filestage - https://www.filestage.io
Frame.io - https://www.frame.io
Frase - https://www.frase.io
Grammarly - https://www.grammarly.com
Grammarly Business - https://www.grammarly.com/business
Hemingway Editor - http://www.hemingwayapp.com
Hootsuite - https://hootsuite.com
Iconosquare - https://www.iconosquare.com
Influencity - https://www.influencity.com
Jasper (formerly Jarvis) - https://www.jasper.ai
Kapwing - https://www.kapwing.com
Later - https://later.com
Looka - https://looka.com
Lovo - https://www.lovo.ai
Lumen5 - https://www.lumen5.com
Magisto - https://www.magisto.com
MidJourney - https://www.midjourney.com
Microsoft Teams - https://www.microsoft.ccm/en-us/microsoft-teams/group-chat-software

Miro - https://miro.com
Notion - https://www.notion.so
OpenAI's ChatGPT - https://openai.com/chatgpt
Otter.ai - https://otter.ai
Planoly - https://www.planoly.com
Remove.bg - https://www.remove.bg
Rev.ai - https://www.rev.ai
RiteTag - https://ritetag.com
Runway ML - https://www.runwayml.com
Slack - https://slack.com
SocialBee - https://socialbee.io
Sonix - https://sonix.ai
Sprout Social - https://sproutsocial.com
Stormboard - https://stormboard.com
Sudowrite - https://www.sudowrite.com
Synthesia - https://www.synthesia.io
TubeBuddy - https://www.tubebuddy.com
Trello - https://trello.com
Upfluence - https://www.upfluence.com
Veed.io - https://www.veed.io
VidIQ - https://vidiq.com
Zoho Writer - https://www.zoho.com/writer

Disclaimer:
This book was created with the assistance of AI tools. While every effort has been made to ensure the accuracy of the information provided, the author does not guarantee the completeness or correctness of the content. The information in this book is for general informational purposes only, and the author assumes no responsibility for any errors, omissions, or outcomes resulting from the use of this information. The reader is advised to verify any facts or data independently. The author shall not be held liable for any damages or losses resulting from the application or misapplication of the information contained herein.

www.ingramcontent.com/pod-product-compliance
Lightning Source LLC
Chambersburg PA
CBHW070956240526
45469CB00016B/1446